Eli. [from old catalog] Huber

Food for the Heavenly Way

Eli. [from old catalog] Huber

Food for the Heavenly Way

ISBN/EAN: 9783744646567

Printed in Europe, USA, Canada, Australia, Japan

Cover: Foto ©ninafisch / pixelio.de

More available books at **www.hansebooks.com**

FOOD FOR THE HEAVENLY WAY:

OR

WORDS OF COUNSEL

TO BEGINNERS IN

THE CHRISTIAN LIFE.

———————

"Follow thou Me."—JESUS.

PHILADELPHIA:
LUTHERAN PUBLICATION SOCIETY
No. 42 NORTH NINTH STREET.

PREFACE.

From the Ten Commandments, as given and explained in Luther's Smaller Catechism, you have been taught the whole sum of human duty, namely, love to God and love to man. To enable you to bear this good fruit you must first make the tree good. In order to do this, you will need the grace of God through faith in Christ Jesus. By what means to obtain this grace you have also learned from the other three parts of your Catechism. You thus possess a knowledge of all truth essential to life and salvation.

But, you possess this saving knowledge as yet only in brief, compendious outline. To fill this out will be your work from this time forward. You want to learn yet more minutely and distinctly what God requires of you, and what through his grace he will do for you. To this end you will need to engage in a life long study of God's Word. To direct and encourage you in this blessed work, is the object of the following address to young Christians. That you may read it carefully and devoutly, is the desire, counsel, and prayer of

YOUR PASTOR.

I PETER ii. 2.

" As new born babes, desire the sincere milk of the word,
that ye may grow thereby."

FOOD FOR THE HEAVENLY WAY.

WE have somewhere read of a ship that had been disabled on the ocean far away from land. When the vessel was at last found, all on board appeared to have perished. Their bodies had wasted away to mere skeletons. Upon examination however, it proved that one of these human frames gave some feeble signs of life. The body was removed and taken in charge by the men of the vessel that had found the wrecked ship. Light food in small quantities was given to it. The indications of life multiplied and became more decided. Under skillful treatment and by means of proper diet judiciously administered, what had been a mere skeleton and had been taken for a corpse at first, assumed flesh and form again, and in due time became a complete, living human body full of grace and energy. But what made this man to differ from his unfortunate companions? Why were they not also taken in hand and restored to health and vigor again? To all outward appearance he and they were alike. They had the same bodily parts

(5)

and organs that he possessed. Why, then, were they not subjected to the same efficient and wise course of treatment, and brought back to beauty and strength ? Ah, there, was one point of difference upon which everything depended. In the case of the one man there was a little spark of life left, though so feeble as to be scarcely perceptible. This was nursed and fed into a flame again. In the case of all the rest this little spark had become extinct altogether ; life was entirely gone. Ah, what a precious thing was that feeble remnant of life to the one man ! What joy and beauty and vigor came out of it !

From this illustration learn the necessity, the value, the promise of the spiritual life, even though it be but that of a babe in Christ. If there be real, genuine life in the soul even though in its feeblest beginning, then there is everything to hope for. Where there is life there is capacity for the reception of food, and where this is there will be growth, and by and by full Christian manhood. Without this new life however you are a spiritual corpse, and all the means of grace in the kingdom of heaven cannot feed you into a growing living being, much less bring you unto the measure of the stature of the fulness of Christ. You must have spiritual life to begin with ; be born again not of blood, nor of the will of the flesh, nor of the will of man, but of God. The step you have taken in coming into the Church of Christ, the promises you have made to renounce the flesh, the world, and the devil, all imply and pre-suppose the new and heavenly life. But there is possibility of deception and we exhort you, therefore, to examine yourself anew whether you be in the faith. And, if you find, as we fondly hope you may, that by the power of the Holy Ghost you have become a new creature in Christ Jesus, then cherish, nourish, develop the precious life you have received. In the words of the text, "as new-born babes, desire the sincere milk of the word, that ye may grow thereby."

GROWTH IN THE NEW LIFE.

In the development of the passage chosen as the basis of our exhortation to you, let us consider the end that is set before you in the text, namely growth in the new life which God has given you, and the means suggested for the accomplishment of this end.

And first let us notice that the object that is placed before you as a child of God is the increase and further development of the divine life begun within you. You are not to remain a babe forever, but to become a full grown man or woman in Christ Jesus. And be it remembered that this is the desire and expressed will of your Father in heaven. He who is himself the giver of this life in its first feeble beginnings is the one who makes it your duty to cherish and nourish this heavenly gift that it may in due time attain to perfection.

"No one," says Pulsford, "becomes a beginner in anything for the sake of being a beginner, but for the sake of being a master or proficient. The beginner therefore in due time leaves the first principles of his profession or trade and goes on to the higher branches." Thus also does our Heavenly Father, through his inspired apostles, direct us to leave the first principles of the doctrine of Christ and go on to perfection, to the condition in which we shall as full-grown men be able to endure the solid food of God's word. We are admonished to grow in grace and in the knowledge of our Lord Jesus Christ. Apostles, prophets, evangelists, pastors and teachers, are given by our ascending Lord for the edifying of the body of Christ, till we all come unto a perfect man, being no more children tossed to and fro and carried about with every wind of doctrine.

Be not influenced to neglect these plain and emphatic injunctions of Scripture by the indifference to spiritual growth that is only too common in all the churches. Not the example of men but the word of the Lord, must be your standard in this matter. It is unfortunately too true, as Pulsford says, that "in religion the highest and noblest of all callings, nothing is commoner than for disciples never to be anything but beginners. They begin very properly with the a, b, c, of Christianity, but strange to say, nine-tenths of them stick there and never get out of the alphabet class." Determine that you will get beyond this class, that you will not remain a babe forever, but will hasten to make of yourself a perfect man, thoroughly furnished unto all good works.

Being satisfied that growth in the new life is a Christian obligation, let us inquire what is involved in this command. In other words, what is meant by growing in this case, and what is it that is to grow.

Growth, as applied to spiritual things, does not consist in increase of size, but in that of activity and power. Thus the mind grows when it increases in intellectual strength.

But to answer more in detail, the growing spoken of in the text means increased power in the inward principle or source of spiritual life ; not merely in some one faculty or organ of that life, but in that hidden centre of our being which imparts vitality to all our faculties. Thus the Saviour says : " I am come that they might have life, and that they might have it more abundantly;" and St. Paul prays "that the Ephesian Christians may be strengthened with might by his spirit in the inner man." What a blessed fact that the central spring of our Christian life, which supplies all the energy required for Christian thought, feeling and activity, need not be exhausted by the constant drain made upon it, but being filled out of the infinite fullness of Christ, may flow on from day to day in ever increasing volume and power!

But this inner principle of life is also to grow in another sense; it is to be developed into all the parts or organs that properly belong to it for its due outward manifestation and for the accomplishment of its various purposes. As from the life in the root there is to be developed the blade, the ear and the full corn in the ear, so from the first beginning of the new life are to be produced all the various parts necessary to its completeness. As an illustration of what is meant and as a guide in the development of your spiritual life, we refer you to that remarkable passage of Scripture found in 2 Peter i: 5-8. Here faith may be regarded as the root or first principle of life, which contains in itself the germ of all the other virtues mentioned. Out of this faith all the rest are to be evolved until all the parts of the new man are completed. Growing, therefore, means exactly what St. Peter commands when he enjoins that to our faith be added virtue, knowledge, temperance, patience, godliness, brotherly kindness and charity. That we may know as definitely as possible what graces must grow out of our faith, a brief explanation of the terms used by the apostle may not be out of place.

Virtue here means moral efficiency, valor and habit in right-doing. *Knowledge*, includes, besides its own usual meaning, the meaning of practical wisdom, or as some one has well expressed it, "the perception of that which the Christian has to do in every relation of life and how he has to do it." *Temperance* is self-control in regard to the pleasures and enjoyments of life. *Patience* is self-control in regard to the vexations and trials of life. *Godliness* is love, reverence, and obedience to God. *Brotherly-kindness* is love to Christians. *Charity* is love to all men. Any one who adds all these things to his faith need not fear that he will be wanting in any one organ of the spiritual life. He will be a complete man as to parts.

The new life having formed all the organs that properly belong to it, there may be growth in each one of these. In fact the same apostle directs that these things are not merely to be in them but they are to abound more and more. Every one of the virtues named in the list is to grow constantly, ever increasing in activity and power. What a combination of manly elements! Faith, that overcomes the world, a tremendous energy in itself; courage and promptness to execute, with wisdom in planning; self-mastery that is not enervated by indulgence, nor discouraged by hardship; and all these supplemented by love, the most powerful spring of action in human nature. What a character, and what power, when these mighty forces are all found in a man and are continually increasing in him! Such a man will never be idle nor unfruitful but will abound to every good work.

THE MEANS OF GROWTH.

Knowing now what the object is that you are to

aim at, let us next inquire how that object is to be accomplished. What must you do in order that you may grow in the life now begun within you? The answer is given in the text: "desire the sincere milk of the word." This is confirmed by what is written in the 5th chapter of Hebrews in which the doctrines of the oracles of God are compared to milk and solid food, the comparison clearly implying that the truths of the Bible are the proper nourishment of the spiritual life from infancy to manhood. The Word of God, then, is the means whereby growth in the divine life is secured. The various forms and the frame of mind in which this is to be received we purpose to set forth.

But before proceeding to this it may be well to inquire what relation the Word of God as spiritual food holds to other means of maintaining and promoting the new life in the heart. Christ calls himself the bread from heaven of which a man *must* eat in order that he may live. St. Paul speaks of a life which he lives *by faith*. The explanation of these seemingly conflicting declarations is contained in the following statement. Christ is in the strict sense of the word the only true food of the spiritual life, and he is received only by faith, and faith is wrought through the Word of God by the Holy Spirit.

That Christ is the proper food of the soul is the plain and emphatic teaching of the Holy Scriptures. He is the way, the truth, and the life; the living

bread which cometh down from heaven; apart
from him no one can bear fruit; whosoever abideth
not in him is cast forth as a branch and is withered.
"He that hath not the Son of God hath not life."
He is to the Christian life what the oil, in the vision
of the golden candlestick in the 4th chapter of
Zechariah, is to the 'burning of the lamps.   He is
the water in the well of Samaria of which if a man
drink he shall never more thirst.   Christ alone has
the words of eternal life; there is none other to
whom you can go.   Says Strutt: "Any attempt to
grow up into Christian manhood without Christ
must result in sterility and disappointment."
Westcott writes: "By the impartment of himself,
his living self, Christ sustains the living man."
Christ therefore is the true food of the soul; "his
flesh is meat indeed and his blood is drink indeed."

Again it is only by *faith* that Christ can be received into the soul. "He that believeth not the
Son shall not see life, but the wrath of God abideth
on him."   Christ dwells in the heart by faith. "In
the reception of Christ faith is the appropriating instrument" (Meyer). "Faith is God's point of con-
tact with the soul" (Pulsford). Faith, accordingly,
is the organ of the spiritual life by means of which
you receive the food essential to its support. By
faith you appropriate the life-elements that are in
Christ, and convert them into spiritual blood, fibre
and muscle. Without faith you receive nothing of
the Lord, however much you may read or hear

about him, or however often you may call upon
him in prayer or come to him at his own table. The
life you now live you live by *the faith of* the Son
of God.

And not only is it true that you can receive Christ
only by faith, but you receive much or little of him
according as your faith is strong or weak. Christ
stands at the door of your heart and will enter in
fully and richly in proportion as by faith, the door
is thrown open more or less widely. "Open thy
mouth wide, and I will fill it." Strutt regards
Christian experience as the result of Christ multiplied by faith, and as Christ is unchangeable, the
product will be proportioned to the strength and
activity of faith. Garbett says: "Faith is the measure of God's gifts to us. The gifts are proportioned
to our fitness and power to receive them. There
are partial gifts for partial faith ; fuller gifts for fuller
faith. The measure in which the sun streams into
a chamber, depends on the degree in which all the
impediments are removed from its entrance. The
limit is not in the glorious orb but in that which receives it. It will enter in wherever it can, though it
be but a broken chink. Throw wide open the shut-
ters and it will stream in till every object becomes
beautiful in its rays. The parted lips of the babe
may sip the honey of the promises, but the open
mouth of the man alone can drink in all the precious
draught."

From the foregoing declarations, then, it is clear

that you live by faith in Christ, and that your life is feeble or energetic according as your faith is great or small. It is, therefore, a matter of vital importance that you maintain the faith you already have, and that you increase the same day by day. Determine, therefore, not to neglect your faith. Cultivate it with the greatest diligence and to the utmost extent.

Now this faith through which alone you can appropriate the life of Christ, is wrought in you by means of the Word of God.

Says St. John: "These things are written that ye might believe that Jesus is the Christ, the Son of God, and believing might have life through his name." "Faith cometh by hearing, and hearing by the Word of God." Christ to be believed on in the world must be known in his true character as a merciful Redeemer. It is by his being lifted up that he will draw all men to himself. This knowledge of Christ is derived from the sacred record. The whole Bible is a witness for Christ, and this testimony, already prepared, the Holy Spirit uses to exhibit and glorify the Saviour, that men may believe on him and come to him for salvation. In the lofty ceiling of a palace in Rome there is an elegant fresco by Guido, the Aurora. On account of its height and position it could not be seen with distinctness nor without discomfort. The owner of the palace, consequently, placed a broad mirror near the floor so related to the painting overhead that you can sit down before it as at a table and look into it at your ease and leisure and enjoy the fine fresco in the ceiling above you. This mirror represents the Bible. You look into it and you see the face of your Lord and the glories of the upper world. The Word of God is the revelation of Jesus Christ, the Saviour of mankind.

The Word of God, therefore, holds an important place in the economy of grace and in whatever form received is productive of faith. Now this testimony for Christ may be given through the reading of the Bible, the hearing of the preached word, or by means of the Sacraments. These all work faith in us and therefore are instruments whereby we are brought into union with Christ. They are the pipes that pour the oil of grace into the heart of the believer. The well of salvation is deep but by the help of these vessels we draw the water of life and drink nevermore to thirst. Set a high value therefore upon all the means of grace; use them with diligence for they are indispensable to you. But do not commit the folly of putting them into the place of Christ. Take away the living branches from the golden candlestick and the pipes become mere empty channels and the lamps, cut off from their source of supply, go out in darkness. Dry up the fountain of living waters and your pitcher returns an empty vessel and a bitter disappointment. The clearest representations of the graciousness of our Lord cannot become a sub-

stitute for the reception of him. Nothing short of
eating the Bread of Life will nourish the soul. The
Saviour himself complains of the Jews, because,
though they had the Scriptures and though these
testified of him, yet they would not come to him
that they might have life. Be not guilty of the
same folly. Remember that all the means of
grace are given to bring you to Christ and Christ
to you, and that you are employing them aright
only when through them you become partakers of
Christ by faith. '' Union with Christ is the end of
all means.''

From the foregoing consideration, then, it ap-
pears that Christ is the soul's true food ; that faith
is the organ or power by which the soul is enabled
to receive him—and that the Word of God in its
several forms is the means by which faith is begun,
maintained and increased. The Word of God is
therefore very properly regarded and spoken of as
milk and meat for the inner man and it follows
that the more fully you receive the same into
your heart, the stronger will be your faith and
the more rapid your growth toward the stature of
manhood in Christ. Aim then at the most com-
prehensive and thorough knowledge of the entire
Word of God. And in the hope of aiding you in
the accomplishing of this noble purpose, the following suggestions are offered in respect to the use to
be made of the Bible :

READING OF THE WORD.

Read it. Read the whole of it—not the New Testament only, but the Old also; nor portions merely of either the one or the other, but all the books in the whole Bible. Do not give way to any notions that tend to undervalue the Old Testament. Do not take up with the idea that it either is not a portion of God's Word, or that, having had its day and served its purpose, it has been superseded by the later and fuller revelation of the New. Do not despise it either as though it were a mode of communicating truth suited only to children or to a rude and ignorant age or nation. Such is not the fact. On the contrary, by virtue of its figurative language and poetic diction it is better adapted for the purpose to be served by it than any other possible mode of presentation, and the time will never come in this world when it may be cast aside as worn out or behind the age. Says Isaac Taylor : " The Old Testament is a book well adapted to the use of all men, in all times, and under all conditions of advancement." Yea, more, as being the foundation upon which the structure of the New Testament was reared, we must study it in order to the proper understanding and appreciation of the revelation made by Christ. Or as Dr. Cuyler has beautifully expressed it : " The Old Testament is the vestibule through which we enter the matchless Parthenon of the New." "All through the Old Testament," says another writer, " the voice and footfall of a coming Saviour are to be heard." And Christ himself declares : " Moses wrote of me." Honor the whole Bible then. Get the benefit of the entire Word of God. "All scripture is profitable." Says Luther: "For many years I have read the Bible twice a year. It is a great and mighty tree, each word of which is a branch. I have shaken them all, so curious was I to know what each branch bore, and every time I have shaken off a couple of pears and apples."

Read the Bible much. Devote all the time to it you can spare. Read it every day. Read it at fixed times. Continue to read it as long as you live. Never lay it aside as a finished book. Said Sir Walter Scott : " The most learned, acute and diligent student cannot in the longest life obtain an entire knowledge of this one volume. The more deeply he works the mine, the richer and more abundant he finds the ore." Patrick Henry regarded it as a misfortune that he did not earlier in life find time to read with proper attention and feeling the book which he regarded as " worth more than all the other books which ever were printed."

Read consecutively. That is, instead of reading now here and now there as chance may direct, read right on, chapter after chapter, in the order in which they stand in the Bible, till a whole book is finished. One part of the Word of God depends so much upon another that it is impossible to get a clear and adequate knowledge of any book in it when it is read in the fragmentary, disjointed method too common among Bible readers. Says Dr. Cuyler: " The Bible is as thoroughly connected and consecutive a work as Bunyan's Pilgrim or Bancroft's History. The whole composition hangs together like a fleece of wool.

Read continuously and much at a time. That is, continue to read without stopping until you have finished a section or even a whole book. The advantage of such a course is, that thus you see the proper relation of the different parts to one another and get the impression of the book as a whole. To observe for yourselves the advantage of this manner of reading take up the account of our Saviour's interview with his disciples shortly before his arrest and read the whole of it without stopping from the 13th chapter of St. John to the end of the 17th. " No one," says Dunn, "who has not made the experiment can imagine what a flood of light falls upon a Pauline Epistle when it is read through at one sitting with quickened attention to its scope and purpose." This method of reading, of course, is not convenient at all times ; but whenever there is sufficient leisure for it, it should be practiced.

Read carefully. Do not read merely to go over a certain amount of ground, but to find out what the Bible says. Read in such a way that when you have ended you can tell what you have read. Mr. Moody says, he used to read so many chapters a day, but that if any one had asked him two hours afterwards what he had read he could not have told him.   He compares this kind of reading to the manner in which he used to hoe turnips when he was a boy.   He says he did the work so badly that he had to put a stick into the ground in the evening to show him next morning where he had left off.   This way of dealing with a turnip patch is an apt illustration of the manner in which a great many persons deal with their Bibles.   In place of this we suggest that you read the Word of God in the careful manner in which Edward White recommends that such master-pieces of literature as Paradise Lost, or Bacon's Essays, should be read, " deliberately, line by line, with the endeavor to obtain, as from a steel die, a vivid impression of each image, to affix a clear meaning to every word employed, to comprehend each argument, to receive an inspiration from every glow of sentiment or gleam of beauty.   Let the mind like the sunbeam dwell on each sentence, until like a flower it unfolds its beauties and its fragrance."

STUDY OF THE WORD.

The object you aim at is to find out the meaning of God's Word.   Much of this you get by the mode of proceeding before recommended.   By it you obtain a general idea of the Bible and become familiar with the sense in which its peculiar terms are employed.   All this is of great advantage and can be enjoyed in no other way.   Yet the Bible must be studied as well as read.   Smaller portions must be taken in hand and made the subject of careful and thorough investigation. Every word, sentence and paragraph must be duly considered, in itself and in its relation to what precedes and what follows. By the aid of the imagination the persons, places and events spoken of in the passage must be called up distinctly before the mind. In the metaphors, types or parables we must from the sign find out the thing signified. There is an idea in every part of God's Word, and when that idea does not at once come to view in the reading we must seek after it till it be found. There are many portions of the Bible that admit of and require this close application of the mind ; that will not in fact yield up their precious secrets until forced to do so by severe and persistent mental effort. Spare no pains then in getting at the meaning of everything in God's Word.

In place of taking up any continuous portion of Scripture to be dealt with in this thorough manner, it is often of advantage to select some particular word or topic, as prayer, love, faith, and see what the Word of God says about it in different places. It helps to attain a fuller knowledge of any special subject in which we may be interested. Mr. Moody thinks very highly of this topical method of Bible study, and speaks in the strongest terms of the beneficial effects thus produced on his own Christian life and character. He says: "If you would only go from Genesis to Revelation and see

all the promises made by God to Abraham, to
Isaac, and to Jacob, to the Jews and the Gentiles,
and to all his people everywhere; if you were to
spend a month feeding on the precious promises
of God, you would not be going about with your
heads hanging down like bulrushes, complaining
how poor you are; but you would lift up your
heads with confidence and proclaim the riches of
his grace because you could not help it. I remember the first time I studied grace, I got so full of it
that I stopped every man and woman I met and
told them how God loved them."

HELPS IN BIBLE STUDY.

The directions thus far given respecting the
reading and study of the Scriptures will enable any
one who faithfully observes them to acquire a very
satisfactory knowledge of the Bible without any
other book than the Bible.

Nevertheless it is a fact that in order to the fullest understanding and appreciation of the Bible
we all stand in need of help from more experienced
and better informed minds. As a result of the
faithful labors of competent students of the Bible
the Church is richly supplied with helps of all
kinds for intelligent reading and study of the Holy
Scriptures. These aids are numerous, varied in
character and adapted to every age, capacity and
degree of knowledge and culture. They consist
of Bible Dictionaries, Concordances and Encyclo-
pœdias, books on the localities, manners and cus-

toms of the East, Bible histories, commentaries, expository lectures and sermons. Besides these, there is much valuable matter published periodically in explanation of the Sunday-school lessons. These helps though designed for this special purpose might be very profitably used by all the members of the Church whether in the Sunday-school or not. Knowing the advantage of having suitable books to aid in the understanding of the Bible we would urge you to supply yourself with a good Bible Dictionary, Concordance and a superior popular Commentary, under all circumstances, and if your means justify, equip yourself with the best Bible aids the market affords. Money thus applied is well invested; it is money spent for the Bread of Life.

Our remarks thus far apply to reading that has for its direct object the better understanding of the Bible. We would yet say a word in behalf of religious reading in general; and that not so much in favor of its profitableness, for that is acknowledged, as to correct a very prevalent notion that religious reading is necessarily dull reading. We cannot waste words, but we do want to assure you in most emphatic terms that religious reading can become intensely interesting; yea that all the satisfaction that others find in poring over the pages of fiction, can be derived from books written on religious subjects. And we feel very sure that if young persons knew the gratification, increasing with years, that may be had from the kind of reading we are advocating, they would never consent to waste their precious time in idleness, trifling conversation, or on unprofitable books. With all the power in us we say, give thyself to religious reading. What Sir John Herschel says of reading in general, holds especially concerning the kind we are considering: "Were I to pray for a taste which should stand me in stead under every variety of circumstances, and be a source of happiness and cheerfulness to me during life, and a shield against its ills, however things might go amiss and the world frown upon me, it would be a taste for reading. Give a man this taste, and the means of gratifying it, and you can hardly fail of making him a happy man, unless, indeed, you put into his hands a most perverse selection of books."

GOD'S WORD IN THE MEMORY.

Remember the Word of God. Make the facts and doctrines of the Bible your own to such an extent that you carry them with you wherever you go, and have them at command whenever you have occasion to use them. The memory is a most important faculty of the mind, and cannot be put to any better use than to be made to serve as a storehouse for the inestimable treasures of God's Word. Whoever has his mind richly furnished with the truths of the Bible, has food for profitable reflection, wisdom for right direction, and motive for sustained action, at all times and under all circum-

stances.   And in thus urging the diligent use of
the memory in the study of Scripture, we refer to
the language as well as the thoughts it expresses.
The idea and the form in God's Word are well
suited to each other, and no better body can be
found for the spirit of the Bible than has been given
to it in the words which the Holy Ghost teacheth.
It is a great advantage, especially in religious devotion and instruction, to be able to clothe our ideas
in the exact language of Scripture.   This habit of
using the memory in the study of the Bible is one
with whose value we are deeply impressed, and
it certainly is cause for regret that the indisposition,
to make the effort necessary to remember the things
learned from the Word of God, is so general.   We
read of periods in the early history of the Christian
church, in which it was quite customary to commit .
the whole of the Psalms to memory, and ministers
particularly were expected to be able to repeat them
by heart.   A certain priest is said to have been re-
jected from a certain bishopric, " for inability to re-
cite the Psalms without book."   Were this still
regarded as necessary to the episcopal office, the
number of bishops would be very much reduced, or
else the memorizing of God's Word become more
common.

DOING THE WORD.

Apply the Word of God in the formation of *opinion*.   Promptly abandon any view on any subject,
whatever, that is at variance with the expressed or

implied mind of Scripture. Promptly adopt and cherish into ever deepening conviction all the judgments of the Bible on all subjects on which it has spoken. Make your faith agree with the faith of God's Word.

Apply it in the cultivation of *right feelings and dispositions.* When we think of doing what the Bible enjoins, we too often think chiefly, if not exclusively, of outward action, as if the feelings of the heart were not a matter of command and prohibition. Such an idea certainly finds no sanction in the Holy Scriptures, for they require special attention to be given to the state of the heart, knowing that out of it are the issues of life, and that good or evil things are brought forth in the conduct according as the treasure of the heart is good or evil. Make it an object then to bring your affections, as well as your faith, into agreement with the Word of God ; resist and suppress all feelings that are disapproved by it, and cherish and cultivate all such as are commended. Take the Sermon on the Mount, for example, and strive to acquire in ever increasing degree the dispositions to which it promises the blessings of the Kingdom of Heaven. Or take the fruits of the spirit enumerated in Galations v. 22–23, and labor to produce them in your own daily life. Or set to work resolutely to put off the things named in Colossians iii. 8-9, and to put on those in 12-15 of the same chapter. It would be well to commit these passages to memory so as to have them before you continually, to direct and stimulate you in the cultivation of a right state of mind.

And lastly apply the Word of God to the production of *right action*. There are many things in the Bible that are not merely to be believed and loved, but they are to be done. You will make a wise and true use of God's Word when you adopt it as your habitual rule to avoid every thing that the Scriptures forbid, and to perform whatever they command. Be a doer of the Word and not a hearer only.

This whole matter of using the Word of God in the production of right opinion, feeling, and conduct, is one of inexpressible importance; and the course recommended, if faithfully pursued, will result in habits and character approved of God and honored by man. There are well-known maxims of everyday life which, diligently practiced, have made many men wise, wealthy, and efficient, and we feel very confident that the purpose to become doers of the Word of God, honestly adopted and conscientiously carried out, would make all men wise unto salvation, rich towards God, and workmen not needing to be ashamed. " After long study and observation," says Alger, " I am forced to believe that the most inveterate and universal fault of men is the neglect to make direct application to self of every practical lesson learned. Only the knowledge which we earnestly obey and fulfill in our own character and conduct is glorified in its

uses for us and for our asssociates." Adolphe
Monod relates the following incident which illus- .
trates in a very forcible manner the blessed effects
of a faithful, practical use of the Bible : " The
mother of a family was married to an infidel who
made jest of religion in the presence of his own
children, yet she succeeded in bringing them all
up in the fear of the Lord. I asked her one day
how she preserved them from the influence of a
father whose sentiments were so opposed to her
own. This was her answer : 'Because to the authority of a father I do not oppose the authority of
a mother, but that of God. From their earliest
years my children have always seen the Bible upon
my table. This holy book has constituted the
whole of their religious instruction. I was silent
that I might allow it to speak. Did they propose
a question, did they commit a fault, did they perform a good action, I opened the Bible, and the
Bible answered, reproved, or encouraged them.
The constant reading of the Scriptures has wrought
the prodigy which surprises you.'" Verily it is
true as St. James says, "Whoso looketh into the
perfect law of liberty and continueth therein, he
being not a forgetful hearer, but a doer of the
work, this man shall be blessed in his deed."

PREACHING OF THE W RD.

Attend the preaching of the Word as God may
give you opportunity. That the ministry of the
gospel is also employed as an agency for the pro-

duction of faith and the development of the spiritual life is apparent from the declarations of God's Word on the subject. Christ commands his gospel to be preached to every creature. St. Paul speaks of himself and Apollos as ministers by whom the Corinthian Christians believed. And the same Apostle asks : "How shall they believe in Him of whom they have not heard, and how shall they hear without a preacher?" Among the gifts Christ gave to men were apostles, prophets, evangelists, pastors, and teachers, for the perfecting of the saints, till they all come, in the unity of the faith and the knowledge of the Son of God, unto a perfect man. In harmony with these Scripture passages, the Augsburg Confession teaches that, "For the purpose of obtaining this faith God has instituted the ministry, and given the gospel and the sacraments, through which as means he imparts the Holy Spirit, who in his own time and place works faith in those that hear the gospel." Says another writer : "God makes use of agency in the economy of grace, . . . and the gospel ministry is the greatest agency that God has employed." As the Spirit of God has seen fit then to make use of the preaching of the Word in the awakening and strengthening of faith, it follows that you must avail yourself of this divinely appointed instrumentality if you would make satisfactory progress in the spiritual life. And that you may be in a condition to derive the greatest amount of good from the preaching of the Word, you must form a true estimate of its value, be guided by correct principles in all your conduct in relation to it, and seek a spiritual frame of mind before hearing, as well as engage in earnest and serious reflection afterwards.

The value of this form of religious instruction will appear from the following considerations :

Preaching is a mode of teaching the Bible, and therefore confers all the blessings that a knowledge of the Bible, however imparted, is calculated to bestow.

It communicates many important religious ideas that in all probability would not reach the majority of the hearers from any other source.

It keeps the subject of religion constantly before the public attention, stirring up the minds of men by way of remembrance, and setting them to thinking and talking about what they have heard.

It gives additional interest to the knowledge it communicates, thus securing closer attention, and, consequently, a better understanding and longer recollection of the truth imparted. This interest is due to several circumstances:

And first, to the nature of the sermon itself. The unity of idea, the clear statement, the orderly arrangement, conclusive argument, and apt illustration characteristic of true sermons, are all calculated to give satisfaction to the mind of the hearer.

Secondly, to the fact of its oral delivery. The

vioce, gesture, expressive countenance of the
speaker all serve to aid in conveying th   ·ing
of what is spoken, and of lending attractiveness
thereunto ; and such a master as Horace tells us
that he who joins the instructive and the agreeable
will carry off every vote.

And lastly, to the accompanying favorable conditions. The presence of a considerable number
of persons, the preliminary devotional exercises,
the hallowed associations of the sanctuary, and the
sense of God's nearness, all combine to impart impressiveness to what is heard from the pulpit.
The Indian preacher understood the value of interest in hearing, who assured his white audience that
they would never forget the fact that they had heard
an Indian preach. . No one who is really in earnest
to acquire a thorough knowledge of God's will can
afford to deprive himself of the advantageous state
of mind produced by the public preaching of the
Word of the Lord.

Another feature of special value in preaching is
the adaptation of truth to the circumstances of the
hearer that is thereby secured. The age, knowledge, capacity, and even the peculiar state of mind
at the time, can all be respected in this mode of
religious instruction. All the truths of the Bible are
valuable in any form and under any circumstances ;
but yet there are times and conditions when one
truth and one particular form of truth are more appropriate and useful than all others. " A word fitly

spoken how good it is." Said a lady to a clergy-
man, who inquired the cause of her dejection, "Sir,
your preaching would starve all the Christians in
the world." "Starve all the Christians in the
world," said the astonished preacher; "why, do I
not speak the truth?" "Yes," replied the lady;
"and so you would were you to stand in the desk
all day, and say my name is Mary." This lady
evidently realized that she had spiritual necessities
that required to be taken into consideration in the
presentation of Scripture truth. Now this adaptation of religious instruction to the particular circumstances of the hearers is just the advantage that
is aimed at, and secured through the preaching of
the Word by a living ministry chosen, equipped,
sent forth, and superintended in all their studies
and labors by the Holy Spirit. By this arrangement in the economy of grace, the right word is
spoken at the right time and in the right place;
guidance is given to them that are perplexed; cor-
rection to them that are out of the way; encouragement to the depressed; consolation to them that
mourn, and warning to those that are in danger.
"Know them which labor among you and are over
you in the Lord, and esteem them very highly in
love for their work's sake."

Adopt true principles whereby to determine
when and where to attend the preaching of the
Word. Now it is most important that all questions
relating to attendance upon public worship should

be decided by fixed principle, and not, as is too commonly the case, left to chance, impulse, or mere arbitrary will. Except in matters of indifference, all a man's actions ought to be determined by some rule previously adopted for the purpose. Thus only will his course of conduct be straightforward, consistent and manly. And certainly the subject of church attendance is not one that is left to every man's own option. Settle upon some principle then by which to decide all such questions whenever they present themselves.

And now what is the right principle to apply when the point arises, Shall I go to my own church to-day or to some other? The true rule undoubtedly is that you ought to be at your own, as over against all others, unless by some providential circumstance God has plainly indicated that he wants you to do otherwise. Whatever advantage your presence gives to a church, you owe to your own rather than to any other. In your own church too, with all whose objects you are familiar, and to whose order of religious service you are accustomed, you will be able to worship God with less distraction than in one which you do not regularly attend. There, too, where your own pastor, who knows you and takes you into prayerful consideration, officiates, you will, as a rule, receive more appropriate and helpful instruction than in any other place. We say then go to your own church always, unless for some reason it has become your duty to attend another.

And what has been said, in regard to deciding where to go to church on particular occasions, will apply also to the other question, whether to go at all or to remain at home.   The true view is that you ought to be at your church as often as it is opened for divine service, unless God by his own providence prevents you.   The Word of God makes it the duty of Christians to assemble themselves together, and the regular and lawful action of a congregation determines when and how often this assembling shall take place.   When therefore a certain number of services have been agreed upon by your church you are brought under obligations as a member to attend them all, unless you are providentially hindered from so doing.   Besides, it is your duty in every possible way to promote the welfare of the church to which you belong.   Your presence is an advantage to your church every time ; it encourages your pastor, increases the interest of others in the services, and helps to attract persons who are not regular attendants.   The uniform presence of the membership of a Christian congregation at all its public services has very much to do with the prosperity of any church. Let but any considerable portion of a congregation be irregular in their attendance, and the inefficiency, if not the dissolution of that organization, is assured.

Again, it is to your interest to hear every sermon that is preached in your church. You know not what you lose by being away from even a single service. Thomas was absent from the little circle of disciples on a certain Sunday, and that very time, Jesus, the risen Saviour, appeared in their midst, showed them his hands and side, and breathed peace and the Holy Ghost upon them. The very disciple whose faith above all others needed encouragement, was not present. How sad the record, "But Thomas was not with them when Jesus came."

Act conscientiously then in relation to attendance upon the preaching of the Word of God; be in your place every time your congregation assembles unless the Lord prevents you, and you will both receive and accomplish greater good than if you allow yourself to be controlled by accident, the feelings of the moment, or the arbitrary decisions of self-will.

Qualify yourself by previous preparation and by subsequent reflection to derive the greatest amount of good from the preaching of the Word. To profit by a discourse on any subject, whatever, the hearer must be in an appropriate frame of mind. The same discourse often has a very different effect upon different persons; yea, upon the same persons in different circumstances. One for instance who longs for the pardon of his sins will listen to a sermon on forgiveness with an intense eagerness, and every word will be to him as rain upon a thirsty land; whilst another who does not realize

the evil of sin, finds the same sermon void of all
interest and can hardly sit still till it is ended. A
right state of mind on the part of the hearer, therefore, has a great deal to do with the pleasure and
profit a sermon will impart.

Now this necessary frame of mind for the profitable hearing of the Word involves, first, a general
interest in the object aimed at by the preaching of
the gospel, as well as in the means whereby that
object is sought to be accomplished. Whoever does
not care for the salvation of mankind, is not con-
cerned for his own spiritual improvement, and has
not learned to find delight in the law of the Lord,
is just in the right state of mind to be indifferent to
the whole business of preaching, and to regard and
pronounce the most effective sermon a piece of
stupidity and an intolerable infliction.

Whatever therefore you do to bring your own
heart to a right state of feeling in regard to the
work of saving men ; whatever you do to increase
your desire to know and understand the Scriptures,
will place you in a condition to derive greater satisfaction and benefit from every sermon you are
privileged to hear. But, besides being in a suitable frame of mind in general, it is necessary also
to be in a right state on the Sabbath day, and particularly before going to the house of God. Like
St. John, you must be in the Spirit on the Lord's
day, properly to appreciate the communications
that are to be made through the Word you hear.

Your mind must feel a chief interest in the occupations of the day of rest, being more inclined to the study and contemplation of divine and spiritual things, than to such as are temporal and worldly. If you allow yourself to become interested in any subjects not appropriate to the Sabbath day, you thereby unfit yourself for the duties of the sanctuary. One subject of real interest excludes all others for the time being. That two bodies cannot occupy the same space at the same time is a law of the mind as well as of matter.

Again the feelings of the heart before divine service must be such as are in accord with the exercises of God's house. A person in one state of mind has feelings that indispose him for any exercise whatever that requires feelings of an opposite character. A parent whose heart is full of grief over the loss of a beloved child is not in a condition to endure, much less enjoy, the voice of music or mirth. The worship of God and the hearing of His Word require feelings of earnestness, soberness, filial gratefulness, and reverential awe ; and these are altogether out of keeping with a frivolous, worldly state of mind. Light and trifling feelings are entirely out of tune with all the services of the sanctuary.

Now this chief interest in spiritual things and this serious heavenly frame of mind depend upon our being engaged with thoughts of a proper character before we go to the house of the Lord. Thinking on a subject awakens interest in it, and begets feelings corresponding to the nature of the thoughts indulged in. This fact then suggests and requires that, before divine service, we rigidly turn our attention away from all worldly things; that we do not engage in meditation, conversation or reading, that will awaken thoughts not of a religious character; but that we occupy our minds with the same general subjects that will claim our attention in the house of God. Read the Bible and books of devotion; engage in prayer for the Holy Spirit's influence; and meditate upon heavenly things. The result of such preparation will be that when you reach the assembly of the saints your mind will be in sweet unison with all the services proper to public worship. From this it is evident that all the employments of the Sabbath day must be of a piece; that we cannot engage in worldly thoughts and pursuits during one part of the day, and then laying these to a side, give ourselves up to the work of prayer, praise and the hearing of the Word.

Sometimes, the indisposition respecting the hearing of the gospel arises from physical causes rather than mental. Indulgence in eating and drinking begets a general sluggishness of body and mind that altogether unfits for the duties of the sanctuary, and inclines much more to plead for a little more sleep and a little more slumber than to call upon the soul and all that is within it to bless the name of the Lord. The Sabbath must not, as is too often the case, be made a day of feasting, but should be one of prayer and fasting instead.

In a discussion respecting the comparative merits of written and extempore sermons, one of the speakers uttered the following sentiments, which, as they bear upon the subject of preparation for the hearing of God's Word, we will quote. He says : " It occurred to me that there might be something said, distinctly in connection with the value and power of sermons, upon extempore listening. I am inclined to think that a great deal of this present craving for special vivacity of manner arises from the listening of the present day being so largely extemporaneous. Did it ever occur to you that listening, in order to be worth much, needs preparing for as much as speaking, and that there are a great many persons who listen extempore who never think upon these great topics, upon which they expect the preacher to speak, up to the last moment of entering the church." The paper from which this extract is taken comments as follows on this same subject: " A good deal is said in these days about *how* to preach. In the days of Christ and Paul, *what* to preach seemed of vastly more importance. How to listen, what preparation of mind and heart is needful, what attitude toward the truth, what appreciation of the truth, these are more important questions than extempore or written preaching. Take heed how ye hear, is a divine injunction ; take heed how ye preach, is a human command. The soil needs preparation quite as much as the sower and the seed."

But as there is a work to be done before divine service, so likewise there is another of equal importance to be performed afterwards. While you are listening to a discourse your whole attention is required to receive into your mind what the speaker is presenting to his audience. So rapidly are the thoughts of a spoken discourse communicated that all one can do is to catch and secure them as they are thrown out. There is no time for any other mental process than that of apprehension. And yet, to get the fullest measure of benefit from what we thus hear, there is a subsequent work to be performed. The sermon must be gone over again after leaving the church, and for the following purposes :

You want to recall the facts and doctrines you have heard, in order, by this effort, to impress them more deeply and lastingly on the memory. Truth, to be profitable, must be remembered.

You want to take up the several ideas of the sermon and think them over again, in order to get their meaning more clearly and fully before the mind.

You want to take up the points advanced by the speaker, and ascertain whether they are true, by comparing them with the Word of God.

You want to consider what there is in all that

was said that in any way concerns your conduct and welfare.

You want to bring back again and hold up before the mind the truths that impressed you in the hearing, in order that these impressions may be reproduced, deepened, and made abiding. Unless this is done their effect will vanish away as doth the morning dew before the advance of day. Pursuing a course like this, the benefit you will receive from the preaching of the Word of God will be increased many times. You hear from fifty to upwards of one hundred sermons yearly on so many distinct subjects. In these sermons, many most valuable facts and Scripture doctrines are presented. These truths, subjected to the process herein recommended, would enrich the mind with most important thought, serve as constant incentives to right and noble conduct, and enter permanently into your Christian character.

PRAYER FOR THE HOLY SPIRIT.

In all your reading and hearing of the Word of God acknowledge your dependence upon the Holy Spirit's aid and pray unceasingly for his presence and guidance. This counsel is based upon the Scripture truth that the Spirit's work is necessary to faith in Jesus Christ. In your Catechism you are taught to say, " I believe that I cannot by my own reason or other natural powers believe in or come to Jesus Christ my Lord; but that the Holy Ghost has called me by his gospel and enlightened me by his gifts." So also does the Augsburg Confession teach that it is "the Holy Spirit who in his own time and place works faith in those that hear the gospel." The Saviour calls the Spirit the Spirit of Truth, and assures his disciples that when he is come he shall guide them into all truth. St. Paul declares with the utmost plainness and emphasis, "that no man can say that Jesus is Lord but by the Holy Ghost." This settles the point as to the need of the Spirit in order to faith.

The precise object to be accomplished by the Spirit is to qualify us to make a right use of the truths made known in the scriptures. It is not to furnish us with another revelation, nor to add anything to what we already have, but simply to enable us to discern and dispose us to receive what we learn from the Bible.

Man by nature is spiritually blind, and in this state cannot know the things of the Spirit of God. Though all the light and glory of revelation were poured upon his sightless eyes, no impression would be produced. "It is nothing that the heavens are opening above until we know what eyes are opened below; as are the eyes so will be the sheen and the glory and the power of the revelation." What Christ did to his disciples that they might understand the scriptures, must be done to men everywhere; and this opening of the understanding is the work of the Holy Spirit.

But, besides being spiritually blind, man is also
naturally indifferent to the things taught in the
Bible; and to many of them positively hostile.
"This is the condemnation, that light has come
into the world, but men loved darkness rather than
light because their deeds were evil." Hence
something must be done, as in the case of Lydia,
to cause them to attend to the things spoken of in
the gospel. This is perhaps the most important
and necessary part of the Spirit's work in the
human mind. Man's aversion to the light in God's
Word has probably more to do with his ignorance
and rejection of Christ than his inability to see.
Two celebrated English divines, it is said, sat up
late into the night upon a certain occasion, discuss-
ing the question whether the intellect or the heart
had the more to do with attaining to a knowledge
of God. A very eminent, learned and able bishop
advocated the side of the intellect, but was com-
pelled by the arguments of his friend to retreat step
by step, from his position till at length, in the
spirit of humility and of candor he exclaimed,
"Then my whole life has been one grand mistake."
Sure it is that seeing eyes are not the only thing we
need ; we must be taught to love the objects that
meet us in the Word of God, before we will attend
to them with the care and diligence necessary to
their proper understanding. And this love for the
law of the Lord the Spirit produces in the soul—
"The love of God is shed abroad in our hearts by
the Holy Ghost which is given us."

And now, as with eyes opened and hearts favorably disposed, we turn to the scriptures, how changed do we find everything in them! To our surprise new objects meet us on every hand, and old ones are seen with greater distinctness and appreciation than ever before. The whole Bible seems glorified. Its formerly obscure pages now appear written in letters of gold; and the entire volume, instead of being a firmament covered with thick darkness, has been changed into a sky brilliant with ten thousand objects of beauty and glory. We find too that we not only see things distinctly and truly, but that we take pleasure in what we behold. As one born blind, whose eyes are opened, enjoys a continual feast, by day and by night, looking upon the beauties of earth and sky, so it is with the heart that has been opened to appreciate the objects brought to view in the holy Scriptures. Such a one finds by his own experience that the testimonies of the Lord are more precious than silver and gold; sweeter also than honey and the honey-comb.

And now admitting the advantage and necessity of the operations of the Holy Spirit in order to faith in Christ, the question arises, How can this help, so indispensable, be secured? We answer, by the cultivation of a meek and holy spirit, and by earnest believing prayer. "Good and upright is the Lord, therefore will he teach sinners in the way. The meek will he guide in judgment, the

meek will he teach his way "—".Though the Lord
be high yet hath he respect unto the lowly; but
the proud he knoweth afar off." "Thus saith the
high and lofty one that inhabiteth eternity,
whose name is holy: I dwell in the high and holy
place, with him also that is of a contrite and
humble spirit, to revive the spirit of the humble
and to revive the heart of the contrite ones."
All the blessings of the kingdom of Christ are
promised to them that are meek and poor in spirit.
He that humbleth himself shall be exalted. Even
a Pagan philosopher once answered the question,
" What is God doing?" by saying, "He is putting
down the proud and exalting the lowly." For a
beautiful exemplification of the grace we are considering, read the prayers of Solomon recorded in
i Kings iii: 6-9. We have quoted so many passages on this subject in the hope of impressing your
mind deeply with the necessity of cultivating the
spirit of humility, if you would obtain in large
measure the presence and power of the Holy Ghost.
In the heart that is filled with pride and self-suffi-
ciency there seems to be no room for the spirit of
wisdom and revelation. " Seest thou a man wise
in his own conceit; there is more hope of a fool
than of him."

The sense of dependence involved in lowliness
of mind will naturally lead to prayer to God for
the assistance of his Holy Spirit, and this brings us
to consider the other condition necessary to secure

the guidance and instruction of the heavenly
Teacher. We must seek the Spirit's operation by
earnest believing prayer. The promises on this
point are many, clear and specially emphatic. "Ask
and ye shall receive. If any man lack wisdom let
him ask of God who giveth liberally and up-
braideth not. If ye then being evil know how to
give good gifts unto your children how much more
will your heavenly Father give the Holy Spirit to
them that ask him!" What a gift and how simple
the condition! The Holy Spirit, to them that ask
him! Concerning this promise Luther says:
"Though we had no motive and incentive to
prayer except this kind and precious saying, it
should be enough of itself." As to the importance
of prayer for the divine influence in the understanding of God's Word, we have full and decided
testimony from eminent servants of the Lord.
"To have prayed well is to have studied well," is a
proverb that has become as familiar as it is true.
Dr. Doddrige says, "The better we pray, the
better we study." "The unction of the Spirit,'
according to Quesnel, "is a great master in
this science, and it is by prayer that we become his scholors." A Latin sentence declares,
"The Holy Spirit keeps the door of the Scriptures.
Admission is not given, unless, conscious that you
are blind, you ask for his help." Of prayer and
study, Bishop Sanderson says, "Omit either, and
the other is lost labor. Prayer without study is

presumption and study without prayer is atheism. You take your books in vain into your hand, if you turn them over and never look higher, and you take God's name in vain in your lips if you cry, 'Give, Lord,' and never stir farther." Luther in answer to a question of Spalatin, "What is the best method of studying Scriptures?" said: "It is very certain, that we cannot attain to the understanding of Scripture either by study or by the intellect. Your first duty is to begin with prayer. Entreat the Lord to grant you of his great mercy the true understanding of his Word . . . Hope for nothing from your own labors, from your own understanding; trust solely in God and in the influence of his Spirit. Believe this on the word of a man who has had experience." That Luther had a most wonderful insight into the meaning of Scripture the world has long since acknowledged, and he himself tells us how he came by it. And his practice was consistent with his advice, for we are assured by one who had every opportunity for knowing that "no day passes that he does not give three hours, and those the best for study, to prayer."

This prayer for the Spirit, however, in order to be availing, must be offered in faith, believing that if we ask, we shall also receive. The Saviour says to his disciples, "whatsoever things ye desire when ye pray, believe that ye receive them, and ye shall have them." St. James, after having directed his readers to pray for wisdom, adds, "but let him pray in faith, nothing wavering." And of the man that wavers he says, "let not that man think that he shall receive anything of the Lord." As everything in prayer depends upon your believing that God hears you, it is of the utmost importance that you learn to offer up this prayer of faith. To this end study the whole subject of prayer; get clear and definite ideas as to what constitutes prayer; fill your mind with the many and encouraging promises made to it, and consider the numerous examples of successful prayer recorded in the Bible. Watch for answers to your own petitions. Prayers are heard, and the answers must somewhere appear, and a little diligence will be sure to find them. One instance of prayer answered in your own experience will beget a conviction as to the efficacy of prayer that the most persuasive arguments of the enemies of the truth cannot overcome.

Learn to pray in faith, then, and when you know how to handle so powerful an instrument with skill and effectiveness, then be diligent in the use of it. Pray when you are perplexed, pray when you are burdened, pray when you are tempted of the devil; under any and all circumstances it is your privilege to send up petitions to God for the help of his Holy Spirit.

Pray at fixed times also. Unless you have your appointed seasons for this duty, you will not pray much. "Daniel kneeled upon his knees three times a day, and gave thanks before God." The

Psalmist says, "Evening, morning and noon will I pray and cry aloud, and he shall hear my voice." Go thou and do likewise.

MEDITATION.

By the attentive reading and study of the Bible and by the diligent hearing of the Word of God you will come into possession of many most valuable facts and truths. These are from time to time to be called up again for further examination and reflection. The operation involves the steady and continued application of the intellect to the topic chosen for meditation ; a direct and attentive looking upon it ; and a revolving of it in the mind to afford opportunity for viewing it on all sides and in all its parts. The result of such a course naturally will be that the truths thus pondered over will be more deeply impressed upon the memory ; their meaning will come to light more fully ; their importance will be appreciated, and profitable trains of thought awakened. This though a most desirable result and well worthy of all the pains it costs, is yet not the chief and ultimate object of meditation. The end aimed at by this important duty is to beget a prevailing spiritual frame of mind, a predominant interest in the truths of the Bible and this with a view to the formation of Christian character. Now this end is secured by serious and habitual meditation upon the things of God's Word. Christian character is the product of Christian thought and Christian conduct. The thoughts

of God as contained in the Bible must be received
into the understanding, loved by the heart and
reduced to practice by the will. From this practice, continued and made habitual, character results. Now practice depends upon conviction and
feeling. The deeper and more abiding these are,
the stronger and steadier will that be. And to
profound conviction and deep feeling, meditation
is essential. Conviction as to truth depends upon
a full apprehension of the evidence that supports
it ; and to realize the force of testimony it must be
duly weighed and considered. Feeling depends
upon the objects we contemplate and the degree of
attention we give them. Any object of thought
will awaken feelings corresponding in character
to the nature of the object itself, and in intensity
to the degree of attention given to it, the length of
time and the freeness with which the object is
permitted to exert its influence on the mind. Thus
the majesty and excellence of God are adapted to
awaken esteem, reverence and grateful love in the
heart, but the longer God's grandeur, worth and
goodness are dwelt upon the stronger will these
feelings become. Now it is meditation that gives
the truths of the Bible the opportunity they require
to work conviction in the soul and to stir up the
affections of the heart. Says John Angel James,
" Study, is to find an unknown truth ; meditation,
is to ponder on what is already known. The end
of study is information ; of meditation, emotion or

practice ; study like a winter's sun gives light, but
little heat ; meditation is like blowing up the fire
when we want not the blaze simply, but the heat.
In study we acquire spiritual wealth ; in meditation we enjoy its benefits." The tendency of contemplation to produce desire and emotion is illus-
trated in the case of the Psalmist : "I remember
the days of old ; I meditate on all thy works ; I
muse on the work of thy hands ;" the result is, "I
stretch forth my hands unto thee ; my soul thirst-
eth after thee as a thirsty land."

This meditation may very often be combined
with the reading and study of the Bible ; or, the
whole time and attention may be given to the un-
standing and fixing in the memory of the portion
of Scripture with which we are engaged, and the
work of meditation be left for some future time.
Often there are leisure hours during the day that
may be devoted to this purpose. Often the duties
with which we are occupied are of such a nature as
not to require the whole attention of the mind at
all times, affording seasons for meditation. Some
pursuits, as that of the laborer, mechanic, or
farmer, leave the mind free much of the time to
muse on any subject that is agreeable. Thus all
will be able to find some time that may be given up
to thought and reflection on religious truth. Or, if
no other season is available, there is the holy Sabbath day that may in considerable part be thus
spent, and all can, like the Psalmist, remember

God upon their bed, and commune with him in the night-watches.

This habit of reflecting upon religious truths previously received into the mind, is one of inestimable importance, and one also whose value is not properly appreciated by most men, and in consequence is too generally neglected. Meditate upon the things you learn from your Bible, give yourself wholly to them, and verily your profiting shall appear to all.

THE HOLY COMMUNION.

That the proper use of the Lord's Supper is a blessing to the participant is the general impression and conviction of the Church, and the testimony of our own writings is especially clear and positive on this subject. Thus the 13th article of the Augsburg Confession declares that "the sacraments have been instituted as signs and evidences of the divine will toward us for the purpose of exciting and strengthening faith." And Luther says: "All the sacraments are instituted for the purpose of nourishing faith." And they have this effect by virtue of the fact that they really are only another form of the gospel itself. Says Luther: "The Supper is a promise of the remission of sins made to us by God; and such a promise as has been confirmed by the death of his Son. . . . Now the Supper is a part of the gospel; nay the very sum and compendium of the gospel. For what is the whole gospel but the good news of the remission of sins.

Now all that can be said in the most ample and copious words concerning the remission of sins and the mercy of God is briefly comprehended in the word of the Testament." The Apology declares : " The word and the external signs work the same thing in our hearts." As Augustine well says, " The sacrament is a visible word ; for the external sign is like a picture and signifies the same thing that is preached by the word ; both therefore effect the same thing." Says Luther again : " We have already said that side by side with the divine promise signs also are given us, to represent by a figure the meaning of the words of the promise." " Through these two things, the word and the external signs, the Holy Ghost operates."—Apology.

Now according to these extracts from Lutheran writings the object of the Lord's Supper is to awaken faith. It has this effect because it is an embodiment of the entire gospel in outward sensible form. That the communion is well adapted to excite and strengthen the faith of the partaker will appear from the following considerations :

The Holy Communion is a combination of all the powerful arguments, drawn from the death of Christ, to show that God is merciful and will pardon the transgressor. Christ died for us and therefore God loved us with a love than which there can be none greater ; by the death of his Son we are reconciled to God and shall therefore much more be saved by his life. God spared not his Son, how shall he not with him freely give us all things? Now the Lord's Supper, as being a shewing of the Lord's death till he come, brings to remembrance all these arguments from the atonement of Christ, and casts their whole weight upon our faith with irresistible conviction.

Again, these truths concerning the remission of sins through the atoning sacrifice of Jesus are presented in outward sensible form, and it is a well-known fact that thought thus communicated is received with greater ease, delight, and distinctness, and consequently also with greater impressiveness than in any other mode.

All these promises, too, instead of being made to the world at large, are given to the individual communicant; and Christian experience teaches that it is a great help to faith to be thus individually assured of God's love and mercy to us, and of our reconciliation with him. The sacrament, as Luther views it, is a direct pledge and message from God to the recipient.

You thus have all the strong warm rays of the gospel-sun gathered together in the Holy Supper as in a sun-glass, and concentrated in their united energy upon the one heart that receives the broken body and the shed blood of Christ. The Communion, however, offers yet another advantage toward enabling the mind to believe in Jesus. All the circumstances connected with this sacred ordinance tend to beget a most tender and susceptible state of mind. You are taken to Gethsemane and you behold the agony of one whose sweat was as great drops of blood falling to the ground. You stand on Calvary, and out of the supernatural darkness there comes the cry of a heart that is broken: "My God, my God, why hast thou forsaken me?" You need not be told whose the agony ; whence the cry; nor yet, on whose account. And as you think of all that was suffered then and there for your sins, your heart, if it be not a stone, must melt with grief. Now then, take all together. The powerful truths connected with the sacrifice of Christ; these presented in sharp outline to the eye; brought home to the single individual; and all this when the heart is melted by the contemplation of the closing scenes in the life of Christ, and you can readily understand that the Lord's Supper is a most efficient means of faith and well calculated as Luther has it, "to tell strongly on the minds of men." You have a clean, sharp die applied with the strongest pressure upon a heart made soft by the touching events associated with the death of the Son of God. With such an instrument and such conditions may we not reasonably hope that the image of the Master should be deeply impressed upon the soul of the worthy communicant.

In view, therefore, of the remarkable adaptation of the Communion to awaken and strengthen faith; we earnestly entreat you to set a high value upon

it, and attend the same regularly and devoutly.
Always make suitable preparation for it by earnest
prayer and meditation.   To this end avail yourself
of the very appropriate and impressive preparatory
service held in our churches before Communion.
No one should fail to be present on these occasions
unless providentially hindered.   Dr. Rhodes in
speaking of the Lord's Supper as promotive of
growth in grace says, "Come, when opportunity
affords, with a loving, penitent heart and a lively
trust, to the observance of the Holy Sacrament, and
be made a partaker of Christ's body and blood,
with all his benefits.   Spiritually eat of the body
that was broken, and drink of the blood that was
shed, and remember the words of your Lord: 'except ye eat the flesh of the son of man and drink
his blood, ye have no life in you.'   The Holy Supper is not only to bring something to your mind,
but to your heart and life and hope.   Make it an
unveiling of the presence of Christ, and it will be
to you what sun and shower are to the drooping
flower."

We have now considered what object you are to
have before you as a beginner in the Christian life,
and by what means you are to accomplish that
object.   The means are of divine appointment,
and consequently cannot fail of their purpose, if
rightly used.   The word that goeth forth out of
God's mouth shall prosper in the thing whereto it is
sent.   The Scriptures are profitable to make the man

of God a perfect man, thoroughly furnished unto all good works. Use the Word of God diligently, wisely and prayerfully, and you will surely have nourishment ministered unto you, and will increase with the increase of God.

That you may employ the word of divine truth as freely and thoroughly as is needful to the best results, you must learn to love it, to desire the sincere milk thereof, even as new-born babes do the nourishment suitable and necessary to their condition. Before you will meditate in the law of the Lord day and night, you must have learned to delight therein. Without a love for the Holy Scriptures, you will not give due attention and study to them. Like children who are constrained to eat what they do not relish, you will not partake very bountifully of the milk and meat of God's Word. Study, therefore, to form a taste for Scripture truth, to form an appetite for the bread of life. It is as necessary to a prosperous spiritual state as a good appetite for the material bread is to a healthy bodily condition.

In order to cultivate a taste for God's Word, read and consider what those who appreciate the worth of the Bible, have said in its behalf; particularly the strong commendation found in the nineteenth and the hundred and nineteenth Psalms.

Think long and intensely upon the objects God's Word sets forth and offers to you. The things of the Bible are exceedingly precious, and the more they are considered and the better they are known, the stronger will be the desire to possess them. The Word of God is sweeter than honey and the honey-comb. Taste and see that the testimonies of the Lord are precious, and you will learn to delight yourselves in his statutes.

Avoid all dispositions, associations and pursuits that tend to beget a distaste for the study of the Scriptures. The Word of God is spiritual in its character, speaking of and commending the things that are on high. To its enjoyment, therefore, a heavenly frame of mind is essential. Whatever is unfavorable to spirituality must be avoided. Companions that are frivolous and worldly-minded, pastimes and pursuits that gratify only the carnal mind, must be given up.

Engage in active service in the vineyard of the Lord. As by sowing and reaping in the fields of earth you acquire an appetite for the natural bread, so by planting and watering and harvesting in the spiritual field you will acquire a relish for the heavenly bread. Enter, with all your heart, into the service of Christ in his church, and you will soon become hungry for the word of life.

Open your soul by prayer and meditation to the influences that come down from the invisible world. Drink in the dews of heavenly grace; let the sun of righteousness shine freely into your heart, and you will experience a hunger for spiritual food like to that which pure air and sunshine beget in the natural body.

Strive, therefore, by these various means to cultivate a taste for the Word of God, and when this
is accomplished, you will need no persuasion to
come to the Book of life ; you will go after it as
naturally and eagerly as the panting hart hastens
to the water-brooks.

But, whilst a love for the Bible may of itself suf-
fice to hold you steadily to the reading and hearing of the Word, yet as a rational being you may
further support your determination to use the Scriptures faithfully by considering the advantages that
result from the growth and energy produced by a
diligent appropriation of the bread of life. And
first and in general, it is a fact that whatever any
man does for his own improvement is never lost
labor. Self-culture always pays for all it costs, in
time, effort, and money. Charles Dickens, in an
address at an agricultural fair, assured the farmers
and land-holders of England that no part of their
holding paid so well for cultivation as the small
estate within the ring-fence of their skull. The tillage of their brains would secure better tillage of
the soil, and thus result in better crops. True as
this is, there is something that pays better yet than
the mere improvement of the intellect; it is the
acquisition of the graces and virtues that constitute
the Christian character, the cultivation of the entire
man—body, soul and spirit.

But, to speak more specifically, spiritual growth
involving increased spiritual power, is necessary to

enable us to resist and overcome the spiritual enemies that are going about seeking our destruction.
An inspired apostle earnestly admonishes Christians to be strong in the Lord, that they may be
able to stand against the wiles of the devil.   We
are living in an enemy's country, and must fight
for our life; and the strength of Christian manhood
is needful that we may not fall in the evil day.

Again, the strength we thus develop makes us
capable of rendering greater service to our fel-
low-men.   Christ assures us that we shall have
the poor with us always, and whenever we will we
may do them good.   What he said of the poor is
true, also of the weak; there will always be such
in the world and strong men consequently are
needed to help their infirmities.   And what is
more glorious than to be able to render needed
service to men for whom Christ died!

The strength you are directed to acquire, is needful also to enable you to discharge with comfort
and efficiency the duties that devolve upon you.
Strength of any kind gives delight in the exercise
of it.   The man of great physical vitality takes
pleasure in bodily exertion, the man of strong
intellect delights in mental effort; so too a man
well fed upon the meat of God's Word will
find enjoyment in the performance of religious
duty. Upon the other hand, when life is
feeble the slightest effort is a burden.   Dr. Hall
counsels friends not to disturb dying persons with

questions, giving as a reason that even the little effort required to say yes, or no, is painful to them. Surely, therefore, the Christian who starves his spiritual life is not in a condition to find much delight in doing the will of his heavenly Father. And what keeps a Christian from finding satisfaction in God's service will also render him inefficient in the same. Christian duty demands the best energies any one is capable of putting forth, and a half-famished man surely is not the one to achieve great things in the Kingdom of God.

Make a strong man of yourself, therefore, if you would not remain idle nor unfruitful in the service of your Master. To be thoroughly furnished unto all good works, you must first become a perfect man.

But beside these considerations drawn from present circumstances and duties, there are others arising out of the nature of the heavenly life.

And, first, you are destined for high and noble companionship hereafter—for the society of the spirits of just men made perfect, and of the holy angels that excel in strength. You want to make yourself worthy of the circle into which you are to be admitted, and therefore you must needs cultivate, to the highest extent possible, all the graces and excellencies that adorn the Christian character. Seek, then, to become meet for the inheritance of the saints that dwell in light.

You are, likewise, destined to an exalted posi-

' tion in the heavenly world that will demand the very virtues and powers you are here set to acquire and cultivate. Whatever notions men may entertain respecting the employments of heaven, you can set it down as a settled fact that there will be something for every one to do, and that of so high a character as to tax his noblest faculties, and call into play his greatest energies.

Again, your real worth, your spiritual attainments, will determine your place in the future world; and that place will be pleasant, honorable, and profitable, in proportion to your fitness to fill it. There are no influences of friends there that will prevail to put any man higher than his real merit deserves. There the best men will hold the best places. " Press toward the mark for the prize of the high calling of God in Christ Jesus.

In view of all these considerations we recommend in conclusion for your imitation, the earnest spirit and purpose respecting the Bible manifested in the following incident: " At a missionary prayer-meeting in Mangaia, after the whole Bible had been received in their own language, an aged disciple, in rising to address the people, said : ' I have often spoken to you from a text out of other parts of the Bible which we had ; but this is the first time we have seen the book of Job in our own language. It is a new book to us. When I received my Bible, I never slept until I had finished this new book of Job. I read it all. Oh, what joy I felt in the won-

www.ingramcontent.com/pod-product-compliance
Lightning Source LLC
Chambersburg PA
CBHW022027080426
42733CB00007B/762